Keeping the Faith In a Doubting World

Karen Demaree

Copyright © 2016 by Karen Demaree

All rights reserved.

This book or any portion thereof may not be reproduced or used in any manner whatsoever without the express written permission of the publisher except for the use of brief quotations in a book review.

Printed in the United States of America

First Printing, 2016

ISBN: 978-1-5356-0424-6

Dedications

In a book of feelings who do we give credit to? Look around you. The people in our lives are responsible. Those are the very people who cause us to experience happiness, anger, shame, embarrassment, hurt, and pain. They can make us feel loved, or they can make us feel unwanted. The person next to you at this very moment inspires *you* in some way. Think about it whether it's in a positive or negative manner. Of course it is up to us to put ourselves in the company of those who inspire and lift us up, but we also deliver the same positive impressions upon them.

My dedications go first to my parents, who laid the foundation of my life. A house is not built without a foundation. My parents determined what the rest of my life would be built upon through their decisions, choices, and actions. A seed planted and nurtured will always grow to be healthy. Our parents plant the seeds of our lives and begin the nurturing process. It is up to us, as individuals, to continue nurturing our lives and making something positive of them, and keep them blooming. Both of my parents are extremely hard-working people. Being one of five children, I never did without. I was in junior high school when my dad was injured on the job and he became disabled. I saw how families can be strengthened through hard times rather than just giving up. I saw my mom step up even higher than expected to help support and manage our family even in the hardest of times. I saw my dad never give up. Those times taught me endurance and perseverance, and instilled within me strength and tenacity. THANK YOU, MOM AND DAD, for planting me on a solid foundation, and for teaching me how to properly *nurture* my life through endurance, strength, respect, loyalty, and love for others.

Children are God's gift that gives us the same opportunity to lay foundations within them that our parents have laid for us. Children are similar to a long-term bank account. After investing time in them and helping them build character as they grow, the investment eventually pays off when you recognize their successes in life and the decisions they make along the way. Those who don't see the return should think back on how much time was invested. My children, Garrett and Leif, two individuals with different personalities, have inspired me in more ways than I can count. Both are in the US Marine Corps. I often think back to their youth and cherish those day dearly, but I am so proud of them now for what they have become and who they are. Stay strong, and always be honorable and respectful to those beside you. THANK YOU, GARRETT AND LEIF, for the inspiration you have instilled in me whether knowingly or not.

    And lastly, to my husband of nine wonderful years. Michael has helped me to enjoy life more than I thought was possible. He never lacks in his support and encouragement. Together we are a team, and together we enjoy life. THANK YOU, MICHAEL.

    I LOVE YOU ALL.

Contents

Introduction xi
Foreword xiv
Anybody There? 1
Too Busy – For Whom 3
Prayer For a Friend 5
Have Faith 6
Little Girl's Prayer 7
To My Brother With Love 9
My Brother's Gone 11
Strength to the Children 12
Reflections of Life 14
Tears to Overcome 15
A Gift of Love 16
She 17
Farewell, Good-Bye 18
If I Only Knew 19
A Cross to Bear 20

Leaning On You 21
Led By An Angel 22
Trapped Within 23
Reminiscing 24
Lost Hope 25
A Lesson From A Sparrow 27
Times of Trials and Suffering 29
In Mother's Arms 30
In Him I Triumph 31
In the Midst of It All 32
Without Perseverance 34
Delusion 35
Delivered From Pain 36
When My Father Calls Me Home 37
Window of Pain 38
Hurting 39
The Miraculous Birth 41
Mind of Misery, Heart of Destitution 43
A Time to Wait 44
Carry On 46

If My Memory Serves Me Well 48
God Commands His Angels 50
A Christmas Prayer For You 51
All Out of Love 53
Cowboy's Prayer 55
Carousel 57
Broken 59
Hidden Tears 61
The Deep In Me 62
How Far 64
Revisted 65
Awakening 66
A Mother's Despair 68
A Road of No Return 72
No Deeper Lover Than This 75
My Love 77
Mesmerized 78
Restless Valentine 79
A Purpose Served 81
My Hope for You & Meghan 82

Waiting on a Call	83
The First	85
My Valentine	86
To You, I Give	87
No One Like YOU	88
Protection of Freedom & Innocence	89
Mostly	91
Always True	92
Where Is Our Humanity	93
Back in the Day	94
All Grown Up	96
Reflections	98
About the Author	100

Introduction

The words on the pages of this book are more than just a collection of words and poetry. Read individually, they would be less meaningful and perhaps not understood. The collection as a whole is my life experience, my diary through poetry. Although I started writing when I was in middle school, this book begins with something from 1980. Each poem is dated and timed as situations occurred, and the feelings, such as joy and pain, were experienced. They emphasize recovering, and achieving joy through sorrow, healing through pain, success through failure, and victory over defeat. They unveil how my faith in Christ has carried me through every situation and trial that I have *ever* faced. Every situation has made me grow into a better person, a stronger person, and, most of all, an understanding person. Every situation has taught me endurance through patience and patience through endurance. I learned to understand before being understood. I learned to give when I had nothing to give, and love when I didn't feel loved. But most of all I learned to be the person that I was created to be by expressing my individuality.

Writing is the easiest way to express my emotions, feelings, and thoughts without the fear of offending someone, or the fear of someone misunderstanding my thoughts and feelings. These were my feelings, thoughts, joys, and sorrows when they were written. These words are not opinions, but rather *my real life experiences,* not intending to hurt anyone, but to release and express myself through writing. People too often, out of fear, keep their feelings and emotions trapped inside and never learn how to express themselves. Therefore, they become prisoners of their own feelings. Once we learn to *face* our feelings, whether they are joy, sorrow, pain, fear, loneliness, defeat, or whatever the case may be, then and only then do we begin to *release* our feelings whether verbally, emotionally, or in writing. And once we begin to release those feelings, we get in touch with ourselves and know the person we were created to be and the purpose we were created to serve.

As I mentioned earlier, I began writing poetry in my early teens and expressing myself on paper. As you read, note the times and dates I mention as they will give you a better understanding of my increasing strength through trials. By overcoming my sorrows, I found joy, and by conquering defeat, I found victory. I have by no means conquered life, but I do refuse to ever give up.

We all have the ability within us to FIGHT. As we continue to use that FIGHT, the energy to overcome situations (but not bring harm to others) will make us stronger individuals and problems become easier to overcome. If we refuse to use this FIGHT, we weaken ourselves and it will become ever more difficult to overcome our trials as they occur. Some of us allow our weariness to keep us down. I learned to rise above, and so can you.

Success is not for those who rely on excuses,
but rather those who search for greater opportunities.

Foreword

I ENJOY LIFE. WHAT I enjoy most is encouraging others. Lifting others when they thought they were at their lowest. Encouraging them when they thought there was no hope. Bringing happiness to others when they never knew the meaning nor felt the feeling. Helping others obtain the "I know I can" attitude.

If I can touch and make a difference in just one life during my lifetime, then I would consider my life's purpose to have been fulfilled. But I seek to make a difference in the lives of many.

What is our purpose or the reason we were created? None of us really know. I am confident that by following your heart, your purpose and plan in life will be fulfilled. It involves living through various feelings, such as disappointment, pain, failure, joy, contentment, love, and success, and through it all our character is built. We become a stronger person. Without defeat how are our strengths ever tested? How do we ever become stronger individuals? If we never suffer defeat, how do we define victory, and without pain, how do we know healing? After all, there is no testimony without a test. If life were simple, we'd all be simpleminded.

The first step in overcoming any situation is accepting that there is a situation that you need to overcome, a situation that you need victory over. We can only seek happiness if we are willing to accept the fact that we are weary. We can only seek victory if we are willing to realize that we, at times, have lost. We can only recover by accepting that we are ill, addicted, or have underachieved. What greater victory is there than to rise above what has beaten us down for so long? That has defeated us in the past? You can and will see victory when you decide to rise above and find your strength from within. We all have it. It's just a matter of wrapping your hands and mind around it. It's a matter of speaking those positive words into YOUR life, and then receiving it and living it.

The poems in this book were, and are, my way of accepting defeat, grief, and weariness. By realizing these situations, I was able to identify a "'place'" in life that I could *choose* to accept or *choose* to rise above. I chose happiness, and defeat has no place in a "happy" world.

If we fail when trying, then we try again and again until we are victorious.

If one reads a poem or two from some of the *dark* days I experienced, you might think I was defeated. You'd think I had given up. But as you continue to read and know me for who I am today, you'll know that I am victorious. I chose to rise above all of the situations and pain I have suffered. I chose to stand up from my fall, brush myself off, and prove that ANYONE can overcome as long as they remove negativity from their mind and heart. Know that you were created to WIN. If this book serves no other purpose than to let one person rise above his or her defeats, then it has served its purpose.

See you in the "victory circle."

FAITH

<u>F</u>inding

<u>A</u>nother

<u>I</u>nch

<u>T</u>o

<u>H</u>old on

Anybody There?

This world is but a mystery
No one will ever solve,
In its little galaxy
It always will revolve.
It cannot speak nor cry for help
No one will lend an ear.
These people give no worry
To things that they might hear.
But for myself, I alone,
Cannot survive on flesh and bone.
Give me more than wisdom,
Grant me more than hope.
Make this day of living
One that I can cope.
Today I live for what I have
For tomorrow there may be
A change in all these problems
To break this bondage free.

Karen DuBois, '80

We cannot begin to coach someone whom we haven't yet taught.

Too Busy – For Whom

I rock you in my arms at night
Until you fall asleep.
I lay you gently down to rest
And pray your soul to keep.

When morning comes I'm rushed about
I'm trying to get dressed.
I can't find the time to stop and play
This house is in a mess.

Your skin is fresh, your eyes are crisp
I long to hold you tight.
But time is passing, we can't be late
I'll hold you tight tonight.

I'm thinking of you all day long
Of how you laugh and play.
I'm wishing I could see you now
But I'm so far away.

By now you must be getting tired
Your little eyes need sleep.
And now you lay your head to nap,
You trust that time will keep.

The day is almost over now
We'll soon be going home.

I have a few things to get done
But you can tag along.

Another day has come and gone
I feel I've cheated you.
So I'll stay home today, my child,
I think we'll see the zoo.

No more days of rushing 'round
Nor putting you aside
We'll spend our time together now,
Together, you and I.

Karen DuBois, 4/84

*At this point my first child was four months old and already in daycare for two months, so I could return to work and support my family.

Prayer For a Friend

I tried to put it down in words
I tried to speak it out.
I even tried to write a song
But nothing came about.

I put my pen and paper down
Not knowing what to say.
I bent my knees and bowed my head
And then began to pray.

I thanked the Lord for giving
Me such a friend as you.
I thanked him for our friendship
And all the things you do.

I thanked him for your tender heart,
Your kind and friendly love.
I thanked him for your guidance,
That comes from up above.

These are the words I tried to write,
The song I tried to sing.
How clear the thoughts when knees are bent,
Our loving God will bring.

Karen DuBois, 1990

Have Faith

God spoke to me with a tiny voice,
"Lift up your head, you must rejoice.
Take the step with faith," he said.
"I will lead you straight ahead."

"Have I been known to lead you wrong?
I'll make the music, you sing the song."
The voice spoke on and told me more.
"I'll lead you through the open doors.
I gave you eyes, of which to see,
A heart, my child, so you'll believe.
And when you learn to trust in me,
Things will happen, you will see."

Karen DuBois, '94

*These words came to me after starting my first business in 1994.

Little Girl's Prayer

When I was just a little girl
Not very much in age,
I'd go before my beside
And bend my knees to pray.
"Dear Jesus, please watch over me
And keep me in your arms.
Give me strength each passing day
Protect me from all harm.
I lift my family also, Lord,
Protect them just the same.
And if they should deny you, Lord,
I'll know you're not to blame."
And now that I'm a mother
With my children next to me,
I go before my bedside
And get on bended knees.
"Dear Jesus, please watch over them
And keep them in your arms.
Give them strength each passing day,
Protect them from all harm.
I lift my family still, oh Lord,
Protect them just the same.
And if they should deny you, Lord,
I'll know you're not to blame."
"And as my child grows
And learns to trust in Thee,
I pray they come to you, oh Lord,

And then on bended knees.
"Dear Jesus, please watch over us
And keep us in your arms.
Give us strength each passing day
And keep us from all harm.
We lift our family also, Lord,
Protect them just the same,
And when it's time to take them, Lord,
We'll know you're not to blame."

Karen DuBois, 1994

*I wrote this two weeks before my brother was killed in a car accident. Unknowingly, the last two lines would soon be reality.

To My Brother With Love

Thinking back when we were kids
Reminiscing all the things we did,
We'd fight the West all alone
And did it all right there at home.

The times we had when we were young
So innocent and full of fun,
I now will have your memories
To be my rising sun.

Somewhere in life we have lost time
Another day has past,
And I can't say where we went wrong
Though I have learned life won't last.

The angels came to take you home
And did not give a warning,
I do trust now you hear my thoughts
As I think of you each morning.

I asked dear God to move the hands
Of life's clock back one day,
And in His solemn words he spoke,
"They only move one way."

Karen DuBois, 9/94

*After my brother's death, I found myself thinking back on times we spent together in our younger years.

When you're lost for words, search your heart.

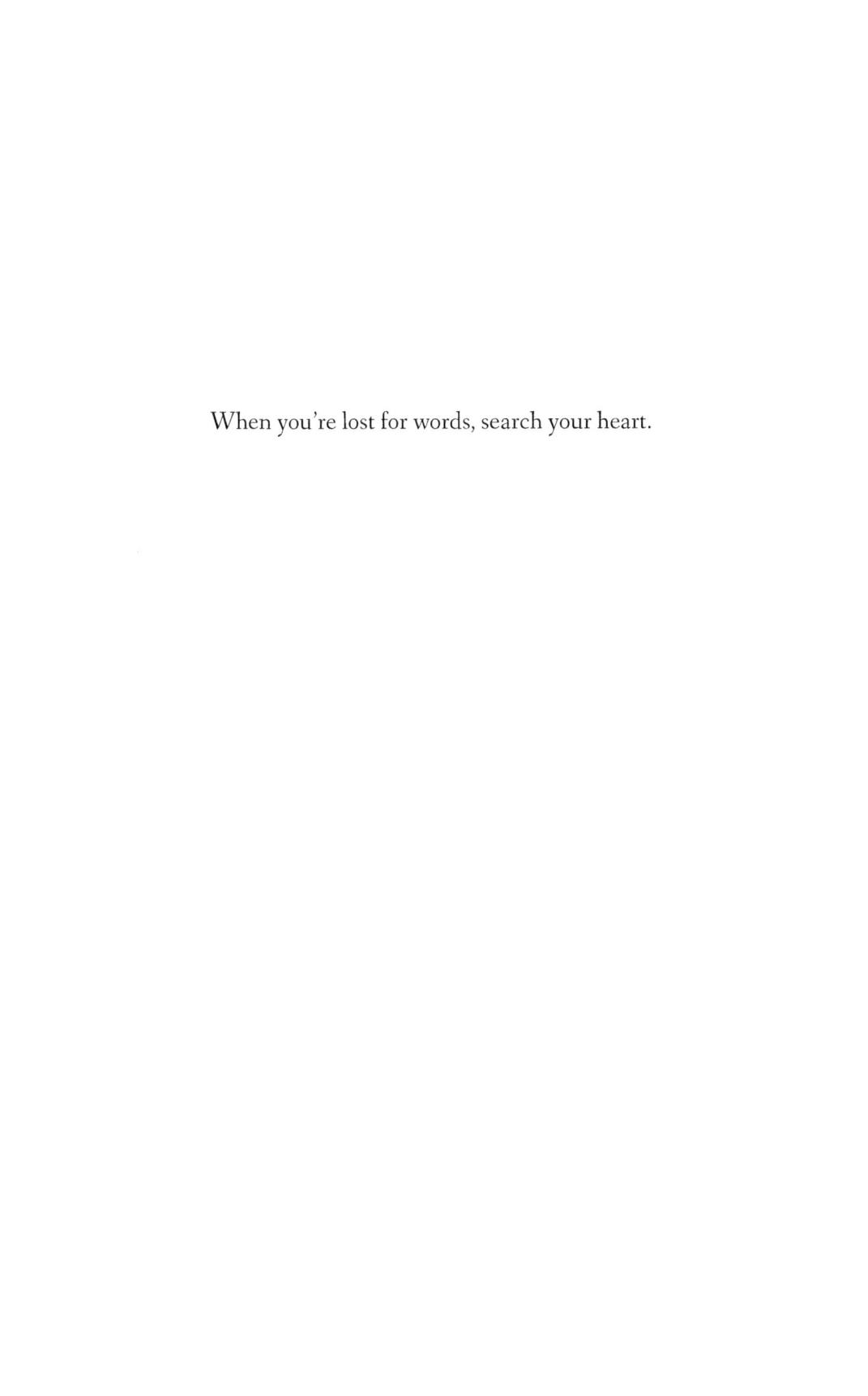

My Brother's Gone

Why must death be so painful?
Why must we feel such hurt?
If birth is surely the most precious,
Why must it end in death?
Why does the world not stop to mourn,
Or feel the hurt I feel?
Why can't the earth pause a while
And everything be still.
Just time enough to feel the pain
And feel the hurt I feel.
For is it that the world cares not
If my hurt will heal?

Karen DuBois, 9/94

*My brother was killed in a car accident September 11, 1994. As with all of my feelings in the past, I kept the pain inside for a long time, making it more difficult to deal with.

Strength to the Children

God bless the little children
Who are born into this world
May your blessings be upon them
Every boy and every girl.

Give them strength, dear God, to walk
The path of which you've paved
Toward the cross, your gracious Son,
His blessed life He gave.

Should one child go astray
As the sheep do in a herd,
Oh, dear Shepherd, lead him back
With strength brought by Your Word.

Karen DuBois, 1/12/95

Nothing will weigh you down without later lifting you up.

Reflections of Life

We put off 'til tomorrow
Of things to do today,
And I, for one, am guilty
Of what I have to say.
To tell the ones we love
How dear they are to us,
To be there when they need us
Without putting up a fuss.
To learn much from our elders
And give them our respect,
For when we then are older
What would our lives reflect?

Karen DuBois, 2/95

Tears to Overcome

I cried ten thousand tears last night
Before I fell asleep,
My heart was feeling so much pain
Those tears I could not keep.

My insides twisting 'round about
Of feelings never told,
From all the pain I hold within
My heart had grown so cold.

When I lay my head to sleep,
I pray God give me rest,
And grant me just another day
To prove my very best.

Perhaps my Lord will use me
As I ponder in His arms,
That soon my heart will not be cold
Yet filled with loving warmth.

Karen DuBois, 10/98

("Weeping may endure for a night, but joy comes in the morning." Psalm 30:5)

A Gift of Love

I thought I'd buy a gift for you
To place beneath the tree,
But when I saw the cost of it
I had to give just me.
Like a piece of precious silver
I may tarnish over time,
But just have faith
And pray for me, my thoughts will soon unwind.
Like a fine perfume I'd buy
The scent may soon grow old,
But I would be, with pampered love,
A friend to soon unfold.
A piece of cloth I could buy
Would soon go out of style,
Yet all the love within me, friend,
Will last for quite a while.
A gift of love is all I have
Though it didn't cost a dime,
But I can say of all the gifts
My love will last through time.

Karen DuBois, 10/98

She...

Once I fell down on my knees
She picked me up with care,
Brushed me off and kissed me,
I'm glad that she was there.

Soon I went to school
To learn my ABCs,
She taught me how to make new friends
And how to fill their needs.

I later got a job
And went out on my own,
Then I put to practice
All the things I had learned.

She hoped she'd taught me well
And now she'd clearly see,
It's not that I could do all things
Just through it all, believe.

Most wouldn't take the time
Or say, "Why should I bother?"
But I can say, "I know she cares,"
Because she is my mother.

Karen DuBois, 10/98
*Dedicated to my loving mother.

Farewell, Good-Bye

My destiny now calls me home
It won't be long before I'm gone.
I can't control my feelings now
Home, at last, is where I'm bound.
Dress me in my finest clothes
Place in my hand a crimson rose.
Sing *Amazing Grace* once more
Before they close the casket door.
I guess I've had a happy life
Though I suffered pain and strife.
I blame myself for what went wrong
And that I let it go so long.
I never meant to cause such pain,
I did what I thought best of all.
Who would have thought I'd ever fall.
You all had faith, thought I was strong,
I'm sure right now you feel you're wrong.
But I'm sure time
Will change the way
You feel about me today.
I hope your love remains the same
Until we see each other again.

Karen Dubois 11/27/98, 8:45 p.m.

*When I thought I was at my breaking point and felt that the only escape would be to give up my life, a voice spoke to me. "Your life is not yours to take." I knew, though weary, that God's grace would see me through.

If I Only Knew

If I could sing
A song today
What would that song
Then be?
A song of joy and happiness?
Where would I find the key?

If I would pray
A prayer today,
What would that prayer be of?
A prayer of joy and happiness?
Where would I find the love?

If I would give
A speech today,
Would I speak on things I've heard?
A speech of joy and happiness?
Where would I find the words?

If I could tell my feelings,
What would those feelings be?
For those of joy and happiness
You'll not get from me.

Karen DuBois, 12/13/98

A Cross to Bear

See these tears upon my face?
Tears of pain can't be erased.
Destitute within my heart,
Circumstances tore me apart.
I put my trust
In friends I've known
But always felt
I was alone.
And then sometimes
I've been accused,
And for what cause
Who would know?
We've all been taught
We reap what we sow.
So is this my cross
In life to bear?
Can anyone say
"I've been there"?
Someone feels pain such as I
And do I have the right
To ask, "Dear God, why?"
If anyone wants then
A chance to choose,
I offer a mile to them in my shoes.

Karen DuBois, 12/13/98

Leaning On You

There was a time in darkness
I knew not where to turn,
And when I thought a prayer
Was just some words I'd learned.

There was a time, not long ago
Just how long, I don't know,
I thought I had all it took
Until I took a second look.

I can't defeat the world alone
Though I thought I was strong,
All my trust in You I place
Comfort found within Your grace.

Touch me with Your healing hand
And teach me, Lord, to understand.
Grant me, Lord, just one more day
That I may learn to trust and pray.

Karen DuBois, 12/21/98, 9:30 a.m.

Led By An Angel

An angel came before me
To lead along the way.
I had the urge to ask him,
"How long are you to stay?"

An angel came before me
As I lie in bed to sleep.
I had the urge to ask him,
"Will you wipe the tears I weep?"

An angel came before me
As I struggled with my fears.
I had the urge to ask him,
"Will you always be right here?"

An angel came before me
As I walked along the way.
He had the urge to ask me,
"Do you hear the things I say?"

"I'll be here right beside you
As you walk along the way.
I'll wipe the tears that you may cry,
I'm here, my friend, to stay."

Karen DuBois, 1/19/99, 7:00 p.m.

Trapped Within

I hold my tears,
I hide my fears,
Won't let my feelings show.
I must be strong,
I must go on,
Who are you that you must know?
I bother no one,
Why should you care?
Why must you interfere?
If I so choose to be alone,
What have you lost so dear?

Karen DuBois, 2/6/99, 8:20 p.m.

Reminiscing

If Merle could sing us
All back home
To the way things used to be,
Back in time
Where we once were
A close-knit family.
I still can see your faces,
A picture captured in my mind.
This picture stays a part of me
Forever, throughout time.
Its seems though we've outgrown
The family we once were.
If only some old memories
Could somehow now occur.
On holidays we gathered 'round
The meals prepared for us.
And now I often wonder,
"Who was TIME to interrupt?"
For death soon overcomes us all,
We'll have no second chance,
And this is all the reason
We must take another glance.
Have we lived life to the fullest?
Thanked our God to whom we pray?
And to our loved ones, each one of them,
To say, "I love you more today."

Karen DuBois, 3/13/99

Lost Hope

When all my fears inside are gone
And all my trust forsaken,
When I've no friends to call my own,
Then what should I partake in?

When the light of day, I see no more,
And darkness overpowers,
When the sun no longer lights my way
And rain no longer showers.

When all the rougher waters
Bring me further out to sea,
And even that "Old Beacon"
Can't find the likes of me.

When I'm as lost as lost can be
And searched but cannot find.
When I have opened both my eyes,
Yet still I feel so blind.

When I have prayed with all my heart
And see no change in sight,
Then I will know that I alone
Am wrong what I thought right.

Karen DuBois, 3/16/99, 6:30 a.m.

When life throws you a curveball, get out the bat. You're in the game.

A Lesson From A Sparrow

I watched a little sparrow
Outside my windowsill,
And couldn't help but wonder
Just how this bird did feel.
I whispered to this sparrow
In a passive kind of way,
"Do you not ever worry
How you will eat today?"
The sparrow seemed to answer
In a meek yet cheerful way,
"In the past my Lord did feed me,
He'll do the same today."
I bent down to my knees
As to look him in the eye,
And I asked this little sparrow,
"Who holds you when you cry?"
The sparrow then looked back at me
And cheerfully did say,
"In the past my Lord did comfort me,
He'll do the same today."
I got a little closer
And I asked the sparrow then,
"But are you ever lonely,
And have you any friend?"
Then I asked the sparrow,
"What guarantee have you?
Do you know with all your heart,

That all these things hold true?"
This sparrow then did sing and shout,
And answered me once more,
"There's no need for me to doubt
The things that I know are true.
It's God who created me,
The same as he did you.
He'll cast us not aside, my friend,
Nor leave us all alone.
You are His chosen, don't you know,
He's been there all along."

Karen DuBois, 10/14/99, 9:30 p.m.

*If we would sit and watch the animals and creatures that God created, and see how they move about with no worries of what the day brings, we would see that they know they are in God's hands and He will provide. We, too, as His creations, should hold on to such faith and know that God will provide and has goodness in store for us.

Times of Trials and Suffering

I wish I could have said good-bye,
I wish I could have stayed,
I wish I could have seen an answer
To all the prayers I prayed.

I wish it hadn't been like this,
I wish you could have seen
The mercies of Almighty God
Set our troubles free.

Perhaps one day you will have faith,
And not only just receive,
For there truly is a difference,
But first, one must believe.

It wasn't all by circumstance,
Nor by some accident,
But by His hand we suffered so
And how our lives thus went.

I still have faith in God above
And trust an answer is still near.
Perhaps it isn't meant to be
That I, myself, be here.

Karen DuBois, 2/3/00

In Mother's Arms

Within your mother's loving arms
Gently caressed to keep you warm,
On that cold and crisp December morn
I recall the day that you were born.
I held you in my arms so tight
And dared to let you from my sight.
It's been so fun to watch you grow
A joy, that now, you wouldn't know.
But one day, son, as you grow older,
You'll have a child to rest on your shoulder.

Karen DuBois, 2/2000

In Him I Triumph

At last, my friend, I conquered all,
I stumbled some, but did not fall.
I put my trust in God above,
God of mercies and God of love.
I sought His face with all my heart,
I knew His Grace would not depart.
I believed each promise of which He spoke,
And trusted this world would not revoke.
I live for Him and no one else,
I rise to Him and die to self.
See here, my friend, of where I am,
Remember, too, from where I came.
And when you feel you can't go on,
Remember I was once the same.

Karen DuBois, 8/27/00, 9:00 a.m.

*He who looks beyond the gloominess of today sees the sunshine of tomorrow.

In the Midst of It All

Upon a cold and dreary day
An old man seemed to pass my way.
I could see he had a need
Just by the sorrow upon his face.
His heart was feeling pain,
The pains, thus, of this world.
Yet, what was I to do?
I was just a little girl.

There was a lonely child
That seemed to cross my path.
A child with no direction
Whose life was fading fast.
A broken home this child had come,
She lived in fear and on the run.
I'd nothing much to offer,
For I alone could think of none.

There was a teenage boy
As lost as he could be.
His heart seemed, oh, so troublesome,
He seemed a lot like me.
Troubles came from every side,
He knew not where to turn.
So I told him of the stories
As a child I once had learned

Stories from the Bible
Of Joshua and of Job,
I felt that all the stories
Would somehow give him hope.
I told him God is there beside us
In ways we may not know.
It's through our faith we'll overcome
For God, Himself, will not let go.

Karen Dubois, 9/4/00

Without Perseverance

If I should close my eyes tonight
And fall into a sleep,
And not awake when morning comes
Nor rise upon my feet,
Would I then rest in eternity
And keep a solemn peace
Of victories I have waited for
Though weary of defeat?
For I was sure that I'd see hope,
I prayed and I had faith,
I'm sure I would have soon received
Had I not stopped to wait.

Karen DuBois, 5/11/01

Delusion

No one knows the shoes I wear
Nor the path of which I tread.
Of treacherous pain and deep despair
From this forsaken life I've led.

No one knows the thoughts
That run through my mind each day.
Of the stressful battles I have fought
Consuming my mind as prey.

No one knows how deep the pain
I suffer every day.
No one knows because no one cares
If I would fade away.

Karen DuBois, 7/01/01

Delivered From Pain

She carried it all
A burdensome load
Years of torment
Not speaking a word.
Heartache after heartache
Hurt after hurt
Till finally one day
She's covered with dirt.
Pain never mentioned
Tears unseen
All covered up
With grasses of green.

Karen DuBois, 8/3/01, 7:36 p.m.

*Some of us keep all of our pain, sorrows, and hurts within rather than release them by talking with someone. Those feelings will consume us and destroy us over time if we let them. I've learned to release those hurts and pain, and chose joy and happiness.

When My Father Calls Me Home

I can hear the Lord call my name
And by the sound it won't be long,
The times are quickly nearing
And I'll soon be going home.

I'll see my heavenly Father
Upon His glorious throne,
What a blessed day that will be
When my Father calls me home.

I'll hear the angels singing
On the golden streets I'll roam,
I'll enter the pearly gates
When my Father calls me home.

I hear his voice so clearly
I know where I belong,
Soon I'll look upon His face
When my Father calls me home.

Karen DuBois, 9/8/01

Window of Pain

Here I sit and gaze upon
The window of my pain.
There's no relief where I came from
It's driving me insane.

No healing words can give relief,
There's too much sorrow, too much grief.
If I could only change the view,
Or somehow all the hurt undo.

Karen DuBois, 10/16/01

Hurting

My pillow wet with tears I've cried,
My heart is ever so broken
Of pain that pierces deep within
From hurting words you've spoken.

You think not of the things you say
And how they cut so deep,
You've even no remorse
As I begin to weep.

Why is it that you hurt me so?
Don't you even care?
By you I birthed our children,
It's your golden ring I wear.

Or am I just a slave,
A prisoner in your home,
That I should be forever hurt
Until my hope is gone?

Karen DuBois, 11/25/01

Weak is the person whose goal is to weaken others,
for their purpose in life is worthless.

The Miraculous Birth

There was a purpose and a plan
That God bestowed within His hand.
To visit a young virgin girl,
And tell her how she'd bless the world.
She would conceive a child of glory.
She wondered, "Who'd believe this story?"
She was a young, unmarried girl,
A virgin, we are told.
She said to God, "You do recall,
I've never married and after all,
I've never been with anyone,
So how could I then bear a son?"
(Gabriel to Mary)
"A child of Glory I will form,
And you will hold Him in your arms.
Yet only for a little while,
For He will be a *different* child.
He'll walk this land to and fro,
He'll save the lost and heal the sick,
And be condemned by those you know.
Yet He will come again in glory
Just as I tell you in this story."
(God to His people, us)
"So then I ask to please be kind,
Love your neighbor and help the blind,
Feed the hungry and the poor,

And count your blessings one by one,
And one day soon you'll see God's Son."
For 'twas the purpose and the plan
That God bestowed within His hand.

Karen DuBois, 12/21/01

Mind of Misery, Heart of Destitution

My lips have hushed to silence,
My heart no longer prays,
I sit and wait in destitution
That God will do just as He says.

The midnight hour falls upon me
And wakes me from my sleep.
Again, I think of all gone wrong,
Again, I start to weep.

There is no comfort anywhere,
I have no peace of mind.
And though I search
The whole world through,
There'll be no one to care.

Karen DuBois, 1/16/02, 8:32 a.m.

A Time to Wait

If I alone in heart's content
Would count the blessings
The Lord has sent
Then I would see
At Heaven's gate
The greatest came
When He had me wait.
He knows my needs
And all my care
He lets me know
He's always there.
He wants to know
That I will pray
Even when I see delay.
He wants to know I'll not give up
Even when He has me wait.

Karen DuBois, 2/5/02

You cannot reach your greatest destiny until
you have met your greatest challenge.

Carry On

Today I walk upon this earth
Tomorrow I shall sleep.
I'm now too tired to carry on
I ask that no one weep.
Carry on the way you would
If I would still be there
Let not my absence slow you down
Carry on and have no fear.

You must live for all your dreams
And see that they come true
I hope that you will never quit
For I'm watching over you.
Carry on the way you would
If I would still be there
Let not my absence slow you down
Carry on and have no fear.

I trust the life I've lived
Before you all my days
Was all it took to teach you
To live in righteous ways
Carry on the way you would
If I would still be there.
Let not my absence slow you down
Carry on and have no fear.

Remember, I'll be watching
So make me proud of you
Every moment has to count
In all the things you do.
So carry on the way you would
If I would still be there.
Let not my absence slow you down
Carry on and have no fear.

Karen DuBois, 2/27/02

*Although still in all of my weariness and lowest of lows, these words sound as though I finally gave up, but I never did. Writing was just a way for me to release some of the hurt and pain from my inner being to make room for faith to restore happiness, joy, and contentment.

If My Memory Serves Me Well

Remembering back when we first met
A relationship that never was
And a love that never grew
That's what my memories recall of you.

A love I thought could someday be
Love I thought could grow.
Though thoughtfulness you never knew
That's what my memories recall of you.

Days of hurt and nights of pain
All the mind games that you played.
Years I wish I could undo
That's what my memories recall of you.

Where were you when tears I cried
And my heart was broken in two.
You never showed your sympathy
That's what my memories recall of you.

Where were you when I retired?
Where were you when family members died?
Where were you when our son was away
And all he wanted was to communicate?
Heartfelt things you couldn't do
That's what my memories recall of you.

Now I think back on all those years
Painful days and nights of tears.
As I try to remember happy times
I can only think of two:
The sons birthed by me and you
That's all my memories I recall of you.

Karen DuBois, 5/20/02,, 7:20 p.m.

God Commands His Angels

God commanded angels
To keep an eye on me,
No matter where I walk
Or where my path may lead.

He commanded even angels
To keep their hand on me,
And if by chance I stumble
To help me from my knees.

He spoke unto His angels
To help me when distressed,
And when I'm feeling weakened
To help me pass the test.

He surrounds me with His angels
From morning until night,
And when no longer clear to me
He opens up my eyes.

"For I will send my angels
To protect you night and day,
And I will always be there
To help you along the way."

Karen DuBois, 8/28/02, 6:20 p.m.

A Christmas Prayer For You

I didn't buy a gift this year,
Though the gift is not what matters.
It's the love you have for me
And the love I have for you,
Along with all the little things
And BIG things that you do.
I often feel bothered
Because you do so much,
But still I am grateful
For my life that you have touched.
I'm sending prayers your way
And if it helps at all,
God answers when I pray.
Look at the times when I welcomed death,
Then he showed me good times
That I still had left.
The times when I couldn't make any end meet,
He promised me victory instead of defeat.
The times that I thought I was left alone,
He reminded me, you and mom are still home.
And look at the times you thought
Your life was done,
He said, "Not yet, I'm not finished, my son."
Before you finish reading
This Christmas gift,

I'll be down on my knees and your names I'll lift
Toward heaven with care,
For you and mom, dad,
In my Christmas prayer.

With all my love,
Karen DuBois, 12/23/03, 2:29 p.m.

*Written for my mom and dad at Christmas.

All Out of Love

I saw a light from heaven
Shinning down upon my home,
And it only took a moment
To know where this light was from.

A light that shone so brightly
A beam from up above,
And it only took a moment
To know it was God's love.

In the light I saw a figure
A silhouette of Him,
The one who bore the pain for me
When before I was condemned.

He reminded me of Calvary
And how He paid the price,
And it only took a moment
To see the sacrifice.

His head pierced with thorns,
His hands that bared the nails,
His side that took the sword,
Through it all He never failed.

To let me know He loved me
He hung there on the cross,

And any time He could have cried,
"God save me from this loss."

But you and I meant more to Him
Than sparing His own life,
For through all His pain and agony
He humbly paid the price.

And now I look upon the cross
To see nothing does compare,
For the price my Lord had chose to pay
That my life would be spared.

His blood has washed my sins away,
His bruises cleansed my soul,
By his stripes I have been healed,
In my life His grace unfolds.

Tis a never ending story
Amazing and so true,
And it only takes a moment
To see He did it all for you.

Karen DuBois, 1/5/04, 9:00 p.m.

Cowboy's Prayer

He hangs his hat at the end of the day,
Removes his boots and puts them away.
He lays his tired bones down to rest,
And knows this day he's done his best.
He hopes to see another day
And so he bows his head to pray.
"Lord, if your eyes look down on me,
I hope you're pleased with what you see.
I trust I've done Your will today,
If not, a second chance, I pray."

Karen DuBois, 2/4/04, 7:56 a.m.

*For my dad, a hardworking man.

Some say the sky is the limit.
I say aim higher for there are no limits.

Carousel

Life is like a carousel
'round and 'round it goes.
The ride you're on is what was left,
Not the ride you would have chose.

The scenery never changes
It's the same as you go 'round.
And you just can't wait 'til this ride stops
To get back on the ground.

And the one that rides beside you
You never get to know,
For the ride is short and when it's done,
You both dismount and go.

Then strangers you remain
Though you rode side by side.
You never got to know each other
On life's carousel of rides.

Karen DuBois, 6/11/04, 9:20 a.m.

When in need of a friend, be a friend first.

Broken

He paces the hall
Like a poor hungry pet,
His sexual desires he hopes
Would be met.
I sleep in our room
Alone in the bed,
He makes himself cozy
On the sofa instead.
I try to be as
A good wife should be,
But my insides cry out
They want to be free.
Enough of this misery,
Torment, and pain,
Enough of me soaking up
His "mind playing" games.
This is hardly a life
A couple should live,
So I'll just move on
And slowly forgive
As I heal from the pain
You've caused over years,
And try to recover
From your inflicted fears.

Karen DuBois, 10/04, 8:38 p.m.

*This was probably the most painful of my poems to write, but I refuse to relive it. Through it all, my heart is filled with forgiveness. And my forgiveness has allowed me to live on with such joy and happiness in forgetting the past.

The tree that bends the most, survives the strongest of storms.

Hidden Tears

In all my deepest feelings
I never seem to cry,
And people seem to wonder
And often ask me why.
It isn't that I do not hurt
Or seem to have no pain,
It isn't that I have no care,
I don't believe in blame.
Look deep within this heart of mine,
Draw closer if you will,
Hold me close beside you,
Make everything be still.
Forsake me not to sorrow,
Choose to hold me tight,
Listen to the tears that fall
As I close my eyes tonight.
And when you see the tears that fall,
You'll know that I, too, cry,
Just not in front of people,
Who often ask me, Why?

Karen DuBois, 2/10/05, 2:00 p.m.

The Deep In Me

Turn my eyes from whence they see
And close them forever more.
For that of which I've looked upon
I wish to see no more.

The troubles of a cruel, cold world
Where no one seems to care
But for themselves they fight to live,
To love, they would not dare.

A show of great intentions
Is always at their hand,
But trouble them with all my hurts,
They would not understand.
A cry for help, I dare not waste,
I'll keep it all inside,
And trust the one within me,
To whom I shall confide.

Karen DuBois, 3/12/05, 6:45 p.m.

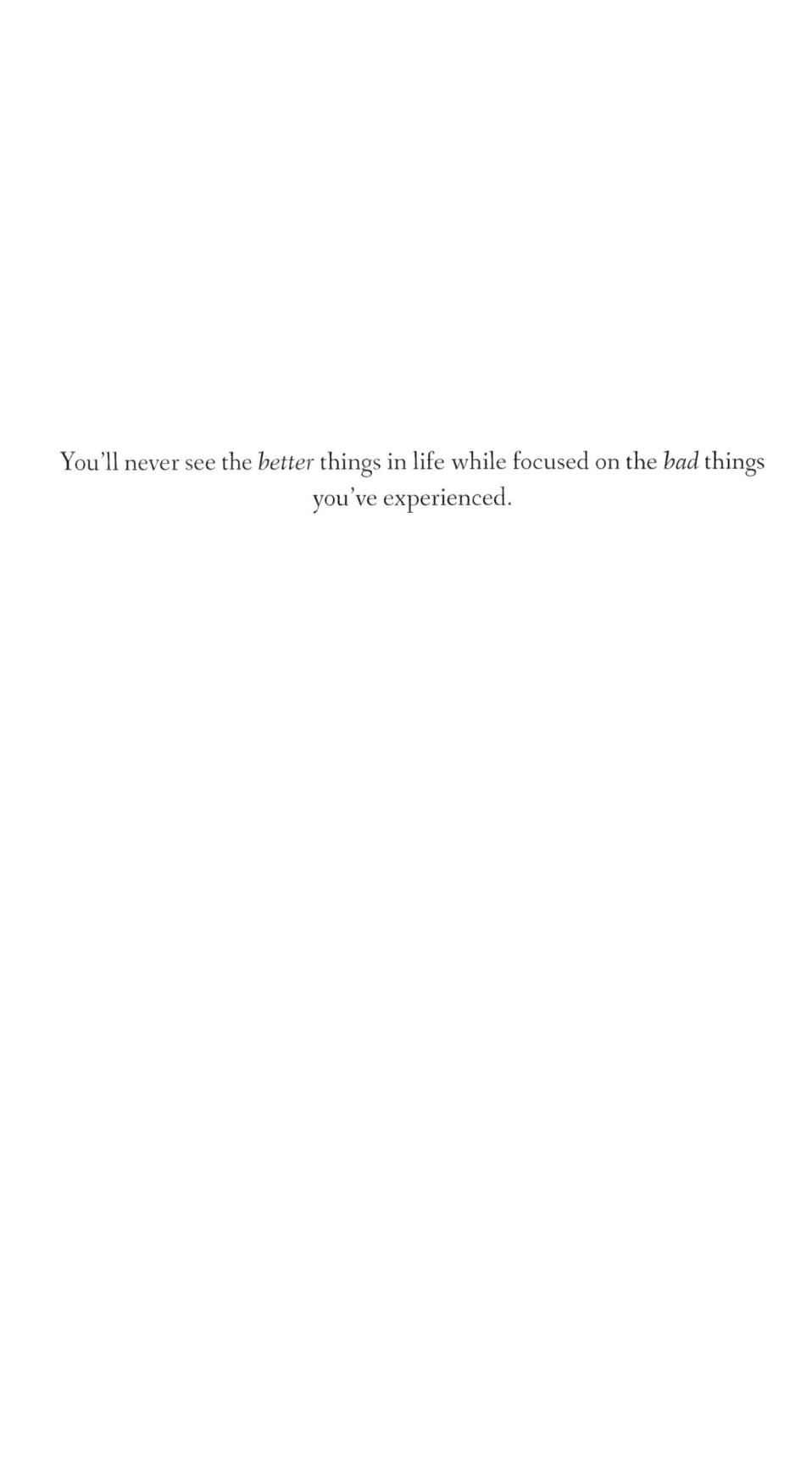

You'll never see the *better* things in life while focused on the *bad* things you've experienced.

How Far

How far am I from heaven
From where I am today,
And do you think, by chance,
That I could make it there today?

If I keep the pathway clear
From distractions on my way,
Do you think, by chance,
That I could make it there today?

If I overcome the obstacles
And temptations on my way,
Do you think, by chance,
That I could make it there today?

Life has so much to offer
It's sinful in a way,
But how far am I from heaven
From where I am today?

If I had to leave from where I am,
Could I get there in a day?
And you think, by chance,
That I could make it there today?

Karen DuBois, 4/26/05, 2:30 p.m.

Revisted

I came to a place
Where I once prayed,
Took my time
With what I had to say.
I asked the Lord,
Whom I so dearly feared,
If he loved me and did He really care.
Unanswered prayers, I've seen enough,
Why must this life of mine be rough?
Why won't He turn His ear t' ward me?
Or even eyes that He would see,
This situation I've been in
Hardly a life I'd ever defend.
He let me speak
'Til I had no more words,
I wondered, still, if he had heard.
And in the quietness of the room
With stillness all around,
As I sat there all alone
Peace and contentment I had found.

Karen DuBois, 6/27/05, 8:20 p.m.

*This time marked five months of a new beginning for a single mom of a loving and compassionate 15-year-old son.

Awakening

Changing times are in the air,
Yet people respond like they don't care.
Cities around us literally falling
While the voice of God is continuously calling.

Fear of hunger, fear of loss,
Survival comes at any cost.
No one caring who they may hurt,
People losing all self-worth.

Are these the signs they talked about
In chapters of the "Book?"
People, stop and give an ear
And have a second look.
Perhaps it's all that we've been warned,
Yet choose to turn our head.
Shall we refuse to change our ways,
And rebel some more instead?

Awake our hearts from their present state
And teach us all Your ways,
Assure us that it's not too late
To encounter better days.

Karen DuBois, 9/1/05, 6:00 a.m.

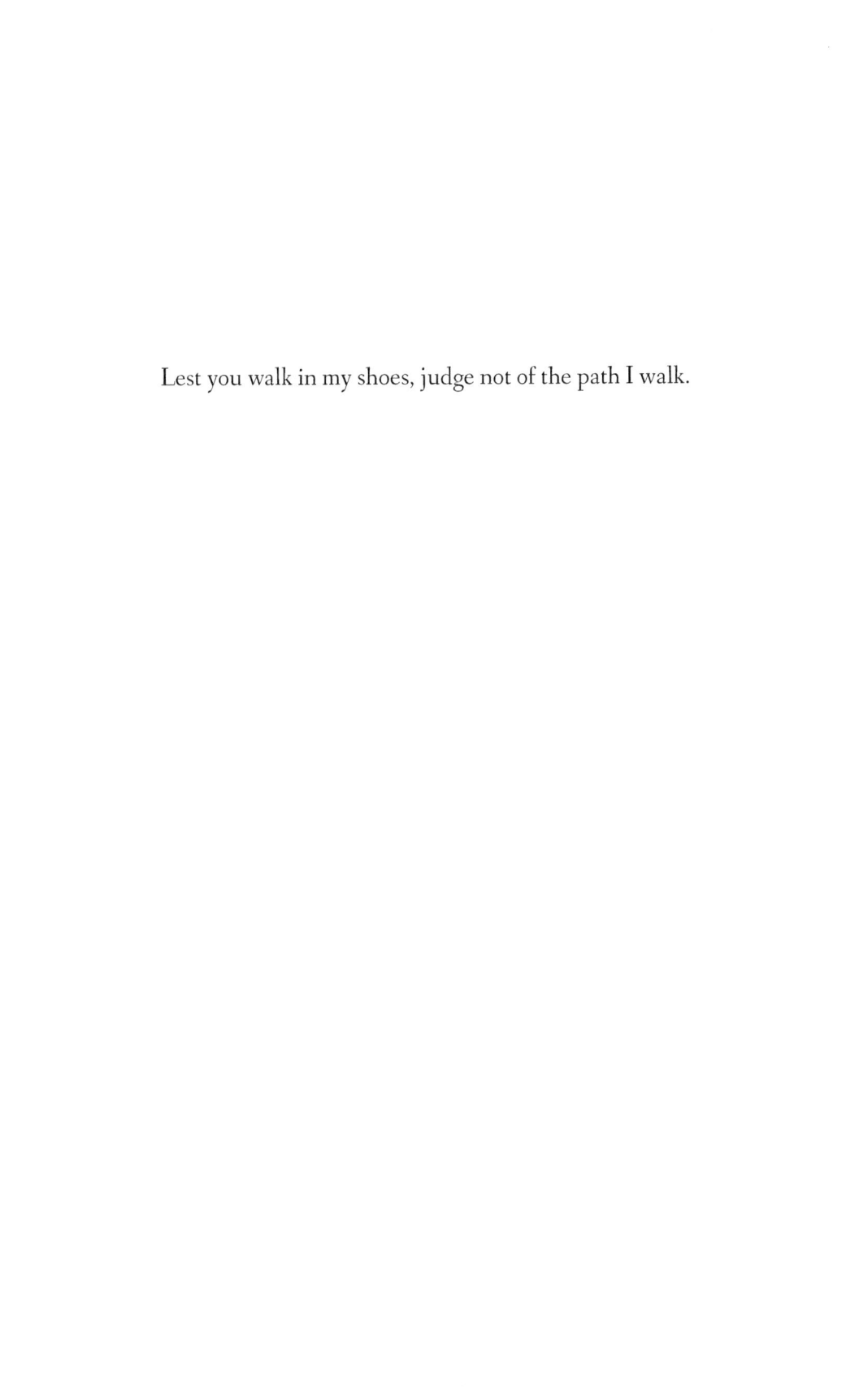

Lest you walk in my shoes, judge not of the path I walk.

A Mother's Despair

What if I begged?
What if I plea?
Would it make any difference?
Would you talk to me?

What if you listened
To what I had to say?
What if I told you
It didn't happen that way?
Since when do you judge
By the things that you hear,
And not give a moment
To lend me you ear?

What if I begged?
What if I plea?
Would it make any difference?
Would you talk to me?

What if your memory
Recalled all the ways
That I was there for you
In every way?
What would it take
To make you believe,
To open your eyes
And get you to see?

What if I begged?
What if I plea?
Would it make any difference?
Would you talk to me?

Rumors and lies
Have filled your mind,
That now you won't give
Your mother some time.
I sit and I ponder,
I hope and I pray,
That you'd sit and listen
To what I have to say.

What if I begged?
What if I plea?
Would it make any difference?
Would you talk to me?

If I were a stranger
Instead of your mother,
Would it make any difference?
Would you still not bother?
You don't know
How this make me feel.
I'm not just somebody
I am your mother, still.

What if I begged?
What if I plea?
Would it make any difference?
Would you talk to me?

It's you mother who carried you
In her womb 'til birth.
Do you think for a moment
I don't know what it's worth?
Remember there's one thing
That never will change,
And that's lost time,
It remains the same.
We can't go back
To capture lost days,
Let not another hour
Be lost this way.

What if I begged?
What if I plea?
Would it make any difference?
Would you talk to me?

Karen DuBois, 9/3/05, 7:30 a.m.

Soft and pretty is a rose,
but when it's cut it doesn't grow.

A Road of No Return

Years and years of struggling
She figured what's the use,
Tired of just holding on
For another one's excuse.
Life had no worth
From where she stood,
She'd change it all
If only she could.
She gave her heart out of love,
But love she never felt.
She did her best of how she played
The hand that she was dealt.

Now a cross marks the spot
On a road of no return,
She'd given up the will to live
From lessons never learned.

She never gave in easily,
She'd fight you 'til the end.
Battle after battle
And wars she'd never win.
She searched and hoped that someone
Would clearly understand
It wasn't just about one's self,
It's protecting where you stand.

Now a cross marks the spot
On a road of no return,

She'd given up the will to live
From lessons never learned.

Those she deeply loved
She cherished in her heart,
And often wondered if they knew
To her what they were worth.
The one's most dear to her
Were the ones who hurt her most.
She didn't care because she knew
What real love really cost.

Now a cross marks the spot
On a road of no return
She'd given up the will to live
From lessons never learned.

Her strengths had finally weakened
From all that she had faced,
She always wore a smile
So she wouldn't leave a trace.
She wanted to be remembered
For the goodness in her heart,
And hoped all would understand
Her reasons to depart.

Now a cross marks the spot
On a road of no return,
She'd given up the will to live
From lessons never learned.

Karen DuBois, 10/23/05, 2:30 p.m.

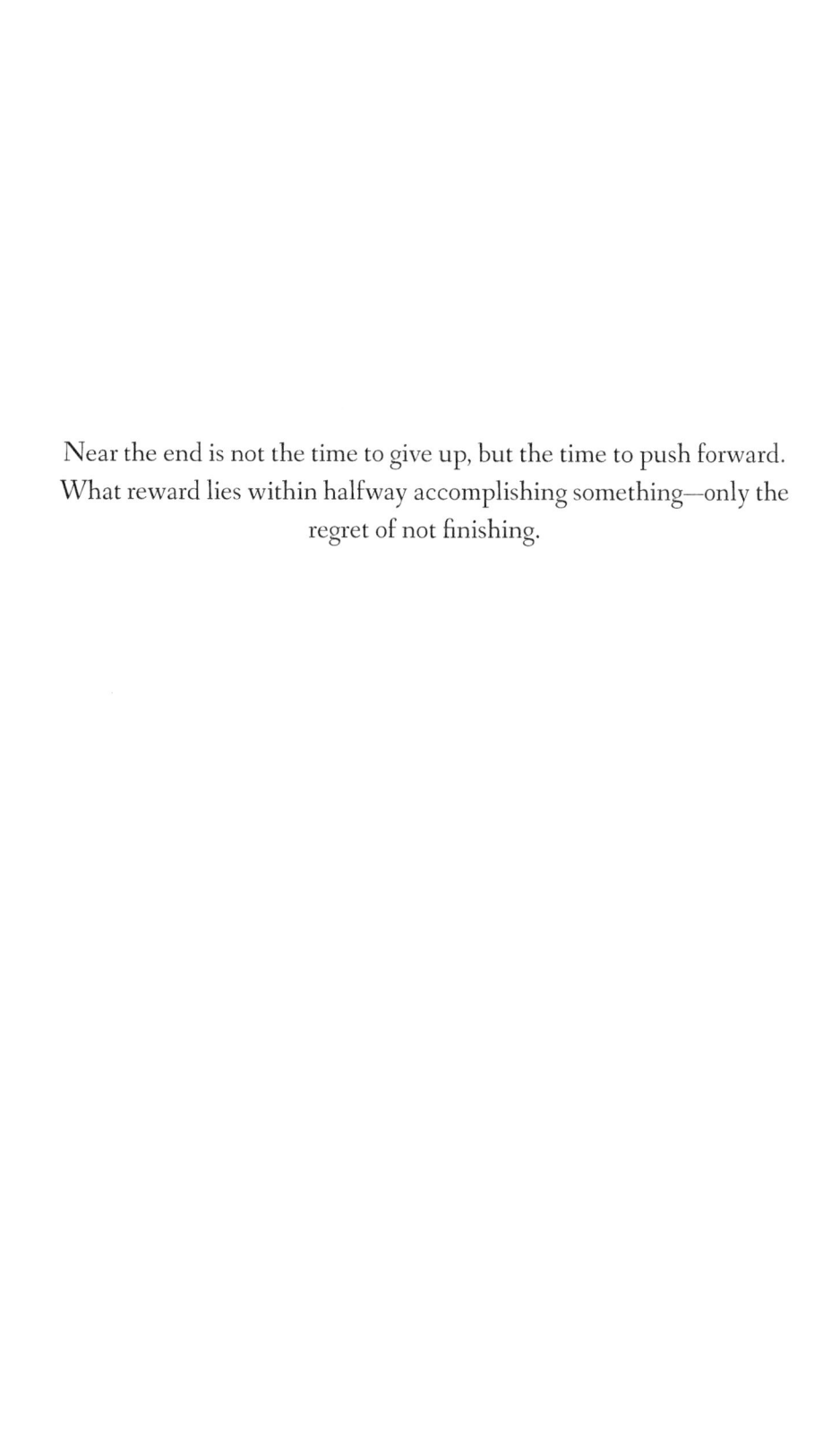

Near the end is not the time to give up, but the time to push forward. What reward lies within halfway accomplishing something—only the regret of not finishing.

No Deeper Lover Than This

I could have searched the whole world through
And never found someone like you.
A perfect love, a perfect match,
A perfect man, a perfect catch.

You make me feel so peacefully free
When I'm with you and you're with me.
It hurts to say good-bye each time,
I hate it when you leave.
I hope you feel the same way, dear,
In that, I must believe.

May our relationship be deepened,
And our love for each other grow,
And the love we feel right now
Be what we'll always know.

Karen DuBois, 7/4/06, 8:20 p.m.

*This was a turning point in my life, a "new leaf" you'd say, when I met someone who loved me back. And from that moment on, my outlook on life was changed for the better.

Expectations are reciprocal.
Don't expect from others what they can't expect from you.

My Love

I could never love another
The way that I love you.

My heart could never be content
The way it is with you.

The sun would never rise nor set
The way it does when I'm with you.

Imagine flowers would never bloom,
Rivers would never flow,
Mornings would never see the dew
If I were not with you.

Karen Demaree, 10/3/06, 7:10 a.m.

Mesmerized

When I gaze upon your baby face,
It takes me to a secluded place.
An island of our own romance
When I glance upon your baby face.

When I look into your blue-green eyes,
I see blue oceans, to my surprise.
An ocean of our own romance
When I glance into your blue-green eyes.

When I hold your hand, it's warm and strong.
It's reassurance of where I belong.
Nestled in your arms alone,
My heart is filled with happy songs.

I love you now, always, and forever.

Karen Demaree, 1/31/12

Restless Valentine

I couldn't wait 'til Christmas
To put this 'neath the tree,
I had to tell you now
How much you mean to me.

I couldn't wait for Thanksgiving
To give my thanks to you,
And let you know I'm grateful
For all the things you do.

I wouldn't wait for Halloween
To give this gift to you,
Should you find it frightful
And confuse it with the spooks.

And though I've worked extremely hard
To put this gift together,
Labor Day just didn't fit
Despite the awesome weather.

July 4th I gave it thought,
But still I couldn't wait.
A day of independence,
It's best I don't delay.

Much too busy dyeing eggs
Right at Easter time,
So here's my special gift to you,
Please be my VALENTINE.

Kdemaree, 2/14/2013

A Purpose Served

Forget me not when I am gone
Nor put my name to rest,
Lest I have failed to leave my mark
Upon my life's request.

We live not for our free will,
Yet designed by God's request,
Forget me not when I am gone
Nor put my name to rest.

If I have failed to put a smile
Upon a passing face,
Then I have failed to recognize
The passing of God's grace.

Though I feel pain,
I shall not hurt,
I'm stronger than the rest,
And all the mountains I must climb
Are simply just a test.

I'll keep my faith
And carry on upon my Lord's request,
Forget me not when I am gone
Nor put my name to rest.

KDemaree, 6/7/2013, 9:20 p.m.

My Hope for You & Meghan

Be not fearful of this day,
Whether there's sunshine
Or skies of gray.
Let not worry
Have its place,
Instead may happiness
Rest upon your face.
For today is your moment,
A jewel you shall hold,
As you meet at the altar
And your vows are told.
Your happiness stands
There by your side,
As you take Meghan
As your beloved bride.
A moment, forever,
You'll never forget.
May each day you recall
The day that you met.
For this is the assurance of
Love renewed,
A relationship promised
And never subdued.
Congratulations. Love, Mom

kdemaree, 10/2013

*Written for my son and new daughter-in-law for their wedding.

Waiting on a Call

Sitting on the porch in the middle of fall,
Got the word you're in town
So I'm expecting a call.
Thinking 'bout the conversation that we will have
Catching up on the past,
Enjoying a laugh.
You're just a busy man...
Doing all that you can.

The morning's gone by and I've no call yet,
I tend to forget how busy you get.
I boast to others of all that you do,
Some people get it, others have no clue.
You're just a busy man...
Doing all that you can.

Days pass by, I haven't heard from you,
I guess you got busy like you usually do.
You can send a text, just to communicate,
Just message me early I won't text late.
You're just a busy man...
Doing all that you can.

I know you're busy living your own life,
Your own kids on the way and a beautiful wife.
Family is blood chiseled in stone,
And we talked a lot before you were grown.

Now you're a busy man...
Doing all that you can.

Time passes on and you wait on a call,
The lack of communication, not expected at all.
You were good to your kids,
You never did them wrong,
They're just so busy, man,
Doing all that they can...

Karen Demaree, 1/14, 7:00 a.m.

The First

Feeling somewhat woozy
As you roll out of bed,
Wondering if this feeling
Is all in your head.
Was it something that you'd eaten?
Maybe something that you drank?
Is there something in the water?
There is no clue, to be honestly frank.
You rush off to the doctor
Who turns to you to say,
"Everything is fine,
You've a baby on the way."
Now weeks pass on
And you're feeling really great,
But then something happens,
Now you hesitate.
Back to the doctor
To see what he would say.
"Everything is fine.
Now there are TWO on the way."

Karen Demaree, 1/22/14

*Written when my son and his wife were informed that they were having twins.

My Valentine

Once upon a time ago,
I met a guy I didn't know.
He gazed a while
Then asked to sit,
I sensed a bit of fun and wit.
He gave his name
And I then mine,
Turns out now
He's my Valentine.
My love grows each day
And forever will
Til the oceans run dry
And the earth stands still.

K.Demaree, 02/10/2014

To You, I Give

I bless you with my heart,
My soul mate.
I give unto you that which I possess.
May inner peace, joy, and contentment
Be your table
As you feast upon
All the goodness life has to offer.
May each day grant you
The success and happiness you seek after,
Along with the birth of a new day to follow.
Forever your love,

Karen Demaree, 7/14

No One Like YOU

You're the light of my life,
The love that I hold,
You're the finest of jewels,
The most precious of gold.
You're the star in the skies,
The light morning dew,
Your hand when it holds mine,
Shows passion of truth.
I could search the world over
And find no one like you,
A man who's so caring,
Loving and true.
You're my loving husband,
My passion is You.

K Demaree 7/14/14

Protection of Freedom & Innocence

A picture of intensity,
Authority and power.
A uniform of courage, honor and commitment.
We see in detail
A symbol of protection, of freedom.
A uniform ornamented with service—
Protection provided to our country,
Our countrymen, and the innocent.
While the red piping, in appearance,
Gives way to rivers of blood shed
For such freedom.
A globe and anchor
That offer no limits.
And the white gloves of delicacy
Held to his chest
In custodial protection.
His own world now, the future,
Of hope and courage.
A serviceman, who
Proudly takes his country into his hands
In defense and protection.
A picture that provides such
Resemblance of security
For his country, for his own.

A stance that represents
"Under my protection,
Under my watch."
Kdemaree 7/2014

*A picture of my son in his USMC uniform holding his twin sons. The picture spoke so much more and seemed to capture a greater meaning than just of my son and grandsons; I put it down in words of how I read the picture.

Mostly

I love you mostly because
You add sunshine to my life,
So you are my sunshine.
I love you mostly because
You make me smile,
So you are my happiness.
I love you mostly because
You are fun to hang out with,
So you are my sidekick.
I love you mostly because
You are friendly,
So you are my best friend.
I love you mostly because
You love me,
So you are forever my love.
I love you mostly always and forever,
But mostly more today than yesterday, and
Twice as much tomorrow.

Karen Demaree, 2/13/2016

Always True

I reminisce to the time we met.
From that time on, I've no regrets.
You caught my eye as I did yours,
Your heart, my dear, I do adore.
Shall we cherish the feelings that we first had
To never fade away as some passing fad?
May I turn your head as I used to do,
And our love stay strong and always true.
May I look in your eyes and always see love,
May we always encourage and never shove.
Shall we share our hearts 'til time is no more,
From mountain to mountain and shore to shore?
May I turn your head as I used to do,
And our love stay strong and always true.

Karen Demaree, 4/21/16

Where Is Our Humanity

Oh, say can you see
all the killing 'round me?
Out of hate and just for spite,
white or black it isn't right.
All the stripes and the stars
have been replaced by broken hearts.
A nation weakened by its own hand
what cause have we
to trash our land?
By strength and honor
we once led,
and how our streets bleed of red.
And, oh, no different
than those afar,
we choose to hurt and inflict pain
for nothing more than a loser's game.
My eyes are red from tears I've shed,
my heart is blue as it aches for you.
Divide us not by religion or race,
let's bond together
through God's loving grace.

Kdemaree 7/18/16 8:00 am

Back in the Day

I remember a land
Of the brave and the free,
A land where people
Cordially said, "Please."
I remember a land
Where we never
Locked doors,
And the young were taught
The basics of chores.
Where the meaning of *respect*
Was clearly understood,
Whether born in the city
Or raised in the woods.
We're losing our value
And core of respect,
'Cause no one looks
Back in the day to reflect.
Rise up, oh youth,
And devote to the cause,
Of restoring our land
To what it once was.

Karen Demaree, 8/2/16, 1:10 p.m.

When we live, we should live with gratitude, integrity, and character.
So when we die, we die with respect.

All Grown Up

My baby boy is now a man
With his bride beside him
At the altar they stand.
A youthful lad I still see
Through the eyes of your mom
You'll always be.
Remember the virtues I instilled in you
To always be kind, loving, and true.
To never take for granted what others will give,
To embrace life's treasures and every day live.
For tomorrow's not promised and will be as it may,
But your future of happiness I will always pray.

Karen Demaree, 8/7/2016 9:35 p.m.

*Dedicated to my son, Lief. I love you.

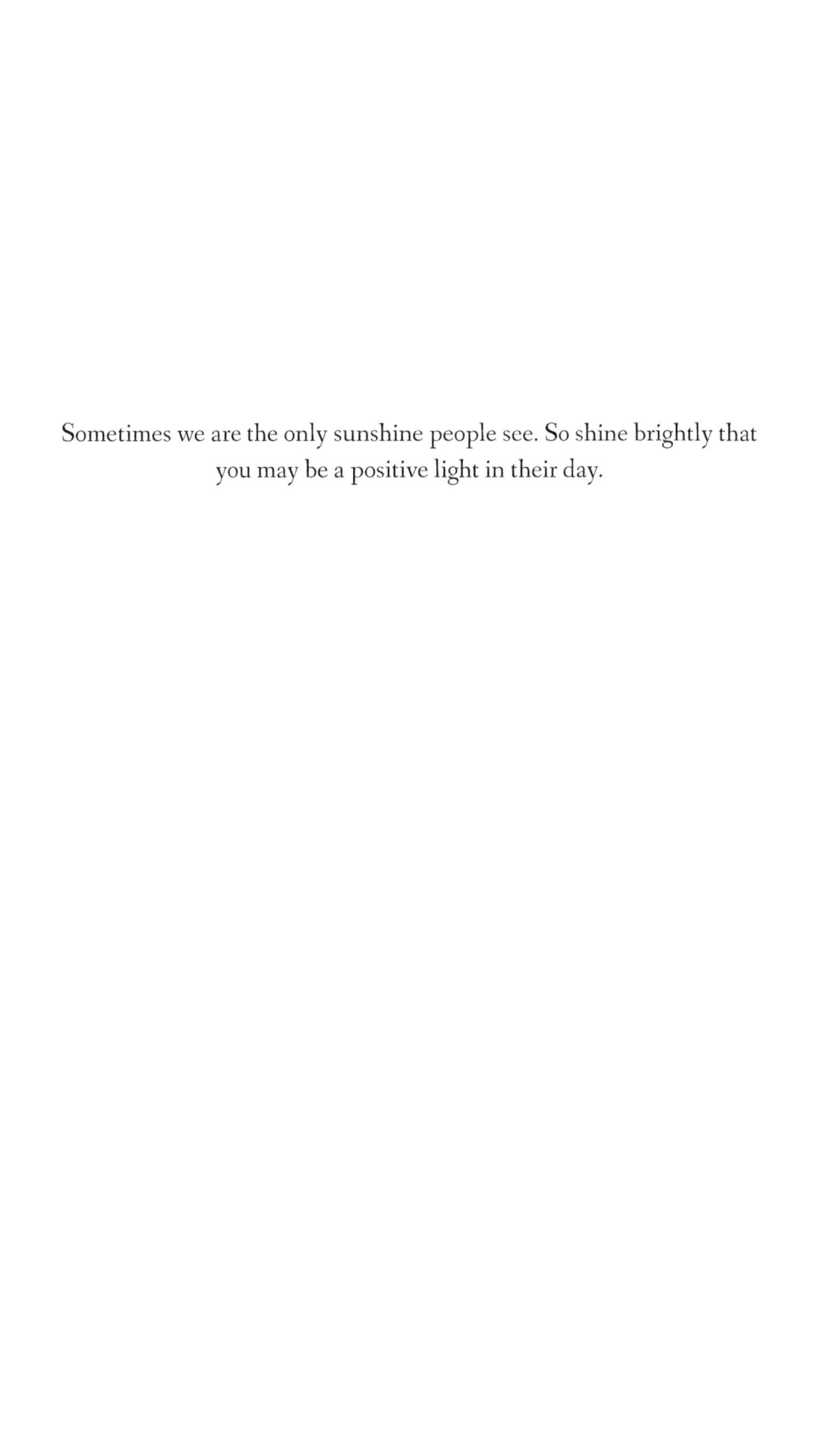

Sometimes we are the only sunshine people see. So shine brightly that you may be a positive light in their day.

Reflections

I hope that after you've had a chance to read my collection of poetry, your heart and life have been touched at some point. My intention in sharing these personal feelings is that others who hurt and suffer heavy burdens throughout life, as I did, will not give up or give in. Perhaps it will now make sense to you with the dates and times in chronological order. My writings are similar to a diary and do not emphasize the situation, but rather release the hurt and pain through poetry. Just as one records in a diary, I wrote a diary in poetry form, and therefore dated my work as I wrote. As I suffered through these situations and expressed myself over the years, I found poetry to be my way of dealing with my problems.

 The trials that we experience throughout life help mold us into stronger people, strong enough that the next trial or difficulty we face we know, without a doubt, we can overcome. Life has so much to offer, and we must accept the bad along with the good because even within the bad there are silver linings. (*Though I walk through the valley of the shadow of death, I will fear no evil; for You are with me.* Psalm 23:4)

 We all need hope. Hope is a feeling of trust. And although there were times I didn't think I had the strength to make it another day, I had hope and trust in God. I stood on and trusted in the promises He gave in His Word. They were intended for me as well as for you. And that hope and trust in God gave me the strength to make it another day, and then another and another until I was slowly brought from the bottom to higher ground. (*He brought me up out of the pit of destruction, out of the miry clay, And He set my feet upon a rock making my footsteps firm.* Psalm 40:2)

 I know there are others out there in the position I was once. I say to you, hold on. Have faith that you are bigger than any problem you are facing or will face. Have faith that you will be a better person in the end. Have faith that your character is being shaped to be a better YOU. (*It is good that one should hope and wait quietly for the salvation of the Lord.* Lamentations 3:26)

Remember, there is never a testimony without a test, and you'll never recognize your strengths unless you've first experienced your weaknesses and have overcome them!

About the Author

My name is Karen Demaree. I was born in a small town in Louisiana in 1959. I am one of five children and enjoyed a very happy childhood. My parents were, and still are, a great and positive influence in my life.

I have been happily married to my wonderful husband Michael for nine years. He has encouraged me, along with my sons, to put my poems out there for others to read, to experience, and to hopefully find something that will help them find hope and strength as I have.

I am a happy and proud mother of two wonderful sons and one stepson.

After twenty-eight years in the banking industry, I have now operated my own business as a consultant for over five years.

I live to inspire others and to encourage those who feel hopeless. I have experienced firsthand some low and weary points in my life, and have had enough faith to overcome and survive them.

I'll continue to "talk the talk" so that anyone can accomplish whatever they put their heart and mind to. With hope and faith, one can overcome anything at any point. We must always see ourselves bigger than the problem we face.

I enjoy writing about my feelings, whether it's sadness, sorrow, joy, or excitement, and expressing them in poetry. I feel it is a genuine way to relate to others who experience similar feelings. I thrive on the opportunity to touch lives in a positive manner. And I trust it to be the purpose and plan that I was placed here to fulfill.

I believe in "opportunities," and that we must all be alert and attentive to opportunities before us. For a missed opportunity today will generate regrets tomorrow. "Don't let today's opportunities be tomorrow's regrets."

Know that happiness is a choice. So choose to live H A P P Y!

CPSIA information can be obtained
at www.ICGtesting.com
Printed in the USA
LVOW04*2122211216
518318LV00006B/15/P

9 781535 604246